GRIP, GIVE AND SWAY

GRIP, GIVE AND SWAY

poems

Kathleen A. Wakefield

SILVER BIRCH PRESS
LOS ANGELES, CALIFORNIA

Published by Silver Birch Press

ISBN-13: 978-0997797206

ISBN-10: 0997797207

EMAIL: silver@silverbirchpress.com

WEB: silverbirchpress.com

BLOG: silverbirchpress.wordpress.com

MAILING ADDRESS:
Silver Birch Press
P.O. Box 29458
Los Angeles, CA 90029

Author photo by Steven Spring.

COVER: "Soulfire" by Steve Carpenter, used by permission.

TABLE OF CONTENTS

I.

II

With deepest gratitude to friends who have graciously read and helped these poems along: Linda Allardt, James Cordeiro, Beatrice Ganley, and Thom Ward. Thank you, Bess Phillips, for teaching me how to sing. To my sons, Tristan and Jesse, and my sisters, Suzanne and Lee, your unwavering love has made all the difference.

For My Sons,

Tristan and Jesse

I say this silence, or better, construct this space
So that somehow something may move across
The caught habits of language to you and me.

–W. S. Graham
"The Contructed Space"

GRIP, GIVE AND SWAY

I

ONCE

The river heaved our boat on its back.
I loved how the narrowness of my life
opened into that prairie of waves, big sky.

One evening we saw the sun's last rays
lift an island from the water; rock and pines floated
mid-air, unreachable mirage hanging

like a painting of St. John on Patmos dreaming
his Revelation: horsemen and scorpion warriors,
sulphurous clouds blackening the skies,

the end of human history revealed—
the river of the water of life flowing down to us
from that place of *no more weeping*, no tears.

THE MUSIC
OF WHAT YOU THINK
YOU CAN'T HEAR

does not trill—
breathtaking.

Put ear to ground.
Footsteps come
and go—lover,
liar, care-taker,
child?

Take time to tell
what's in or out
of tune.

Worms masquerade
as moving dirt,
tiny quakes for which
an earthy damp's
required.

Roots hum rumors
of a spring below
fierce enough
to strike from rock

unruly songs
that might be
moan, plain howl,
nothing beautiful.

A crowd is not
required for singing
the necessary song.

TO BEGIN WITH

I am going to lie down in the field,
grass a green halo over my head.

I'll let the sun singe the peach,
my flesh, luxurious, ruined.

Let rain have its way with me
so I can feel my mother's washcloth

on my face, hand I turned from.
Lord soften the hard pit of my heart.

Excuse me, grass, for keeping
you in the dark while I lie here

considering what I will,
and will not say.

THE OTHER SIDE

Now that I'm on the other side of the river
I wave back at you and the house I once
knew on the road where I no longer live.
Good-bye old life, hello to the new, though
little's changed except where I lay my pillow
and the view from this front window. I have
a streetlight now. It shines pink on snow.
A corner store. Now and then the furnace
chuffs. Clocks tick as if pushing reluctant
seconds aside to see what's next. A guest,
I grieve over what I'd hardly owned, lucky
to be here by this river, exact in its shining.

HE ADMITS TO ASTONISHMENT

I admit to astonishment at the sparrows
nesting in the ivy outside the kitchen window,
trying to usher in new life this late in the year.
I don't like the way they flutter madly to hold themselves up.
They remind me how hard it is to bear the weight of who I am.

That day you brought a pomegranate home
we stared at that strange fruit until you cut it open. Marvelous sweet,
but I did not like how the seeds broke and spit between my teeth.
I suppose it's always been hard for me to take in
much joy for fear of falling down.

Some say I was a reckless man,
but for you I held a tenderness left unspoken.
I've known little of forgiveness, and I'll not lay claim to yours.
The minister you liked said, *God's grace is already yours*,
but I feel nettles turning inside me, and I know it's not
my heart and lungs failing, though some days
I find it hard to breathe. I say I'll go
the day I turn this darkness out of me.

RELIQUARY

> *He turned around in the crowd*
> *and asked, "Who touched my cloak?"*
>
> –Mark 5: 30

Begin with bone.
        A shaving, shards. Tibia,
                femur, scapula, skull.

Washed up. Exhumed.
        Stolen. Wrapped in muslin
                then housed in carved ivory,

hammered gold. True.
        Not true. A sham. Shameful,
                these drops of Mary's milk

in a vial. Christ's fingernails. Bits
        of St. Oda that might be the bones of
                beggar or fox.

True, the seeping wound,
        grief housed in living bone.
                When the Count of Flanders

ordered St. Ursmer's relics brought
        before his feuding knights, tears
                watered their beards.

FATHER TO SON

I'm not one to believe in angels and such.
I suppose it's just plain tenderness folks want
from a God too high and mighty for them.
I believe in what I see, so who am I to talk?

Whatever your mother saw that day
between the back shed and the Mercer's lot
where I tuck the grass clippings to richen
she wouldn't say exactly, only that
"I've seen the Lord, or one of his kind."

Then she went about her business calm as could be.
I admit I feared for her state of mind
and watched her like a child, but not for long.
Why, she was more herself than ever.
Her kindness only deepened and the way
of her patience which could drive a person crazy.

You know what I mean, living in that house.
Whatever you saw at the end, that's just
what happens to folks when they get there.
I'm telling you these things because you never
know what passes from one generation
to the next. That way of *seeing*, I mean.
I wouldn't want you to be distressed
if you saw something different in this world
than maybe you expected.

Like I said, I believe in what I see.
Your mother was my eye for God.
I've got to wash that damn dog now.
He got into something wicked in those woods
for the pure joy of it. Then I'll stake up
the new Sunburst tomatoes I'm trying this year.
I swear they'd groan if they could
under their newfound weight and shine.
I'll be sure to save some for you the next time you come by.

YNGKILING

"Middle English 'yngkiling' whisper, mention,
probably from 'inclen' to hint at; akin
to Old English 'inca' suspicion."

—merriam-webster.com

You've heard of though never seen the inkling:
one-legged, tiny, long-lashed creature
who with its one eye peers
around the corner.

Easy to dismiss—
hint, intimation, vague notion,
call it what you like. While it may not
have the longer, larger view,
the inkling says,
beware of false sources.

Inklings are not angels.
They will not lift you up
nor set you on the right path.
Here and gone—
skin-shiver, sigh, sliver of light.
In this regard, angel and inkling are alike.

I had an inkling this would happen, you say,
having already brushed from
your shoulder or the curve of your ear
toes curled on the brink
of revelation.

ADMISSIBLE EVIDENCE

-Epipactus latifolia,
  family orchidacea

One stalk leaves wrap around
like rungs on a small spiral staircase.
Note the thick, pointed buds, immodestly erect.
From above, the whole thing was nearly missed,
for days misidentified until it bloomed
from the lowest bud upward.
Something to do with sex.

The pink flowers droop bell-like.
Bend down, lift one up and they're really sepals
framing a face. The full bottomed lower lip,
violet tinted, opens to a mouth of dark maroon, sticky, wet.
The upper sepal's a mask, gold eyes
luring a dancer to the dance. Fox trot, waltz?
No, tango:
              this is the broad-leafed helleborine,
rhizomous, considered a nuisance for its spreading habit,
assumed hermaphroditic. So low to the ground
one must crouch to see the clumsily
tilted head, threadlike hands, wings fitted
to a body with tongue enough
to name the taste.

GOOD FRIDAY

In that hour when everything crept into the mouth of nothing,
the head on the pillow and the fist, the broom tree
and cedar, all seven days; fox, gazelle, the wild bull, seahorse and worm;
wheels and gunfire; banknotes, stars, pillars of stone
and ash, all the hidden forms of mercy;
night and day.

In that hour the consolation of spring fed rivers, glacial pools and wadis
vanished, and the chorales of galaxies and shore birds also.
The recitation of psalms ceased,
the names of things were hidden away,
their numbers and signs.

In that hour the void stammered,
neither pit nor cave nor abyss but emptiness
darker than a wilderness without the storm of creation.

I KNEW YOU LONG ENOUGH TO KNOW

Mornings we walked the dog to the muskrats' lodge
erupting from the pond's silver skin,
dry cattails piled every which way in mud,
house and food for the winter.

I've watched them night swimming in the St. Lawrence,
from each small head a wake spreading
into ripples of black silk.

Some days you went north, as if remembering
the weight of a harsh hand on your shoulder.
I learned not to follow you there,
not if I wanted to see you at supper.
If I wanted to see you.

I knew you long enough to know
you didn't believe in a life lived at the end of a leash.
Letting that dog go free got you in trouble
more times than I want to say.

TO CLARA, A REHEARSAL

> *Die lieder sind verweht . . .*
> ("The songs trail away in the wind")
> — *O Kuhler Wald (text by Clemens Maria Wenzeslau von Brentano)*
> Johannes Brahms, *Opus 72, no. 3*

I am sorry to disturb you so late in the evening.
You see, I'd forgotten to say what I came for earlier.
It is lovely tonight, isn't it? The soft rushing
of wind through the leaves before they turn
incites the air with misgivings about the season.
No, I suppose the air feels nothing.

There are as many ways to end a story
as there are to end a day,
with the awaited storm, agitation
that alternately lifts the soul up, then terrifies,
or the slow blue hours of nightfall, coolness
that seems less like something falling on earth
than something taken away.

I never believed in falling in love.
I've known too much of the tyranny of lust.
Yet my hand can scarcely come near your wrist
without the trembling of sinews that have caressed ivory keys.
This wave of tenderness strangles the heart.
Where else can it go to but there?

Surely you must know how I feel.
I give these notes to the voice of another
when always it is what *I* feel,
your coming close, then drifting away . . .
Let us walk awhile under the dimming streetlights
in sober introspection. About these songs,
bodiless words and music speaking to each other.

THE REV. DR. ROBERT WALKER SKATING ON DUDDINGSTON LOCH

—Portrait in oil, Sir Henry Raeburn, c. 1795

I'd like to think it's late Saturday afternoon, sky on fire,
sermon finished, and he's happy to be skating
alone, the village children gathered in for early supper and bed.
Then again, this might be a method of composing
just shy of dancing's pleasure.

Dressed in black skates with red laces,
black leggings and coat, wide-brimmed black top hat
tipped back from flushed cheeks and pointed nose,
he cuts a fine figure against the green ice,
one leg swept up behind him, arms folded across his chest.

Drawn, it seems, by his steady gaze, does he lean
toward thoughts of the heaven he hopes for,
or the house ahead and his supper?
He'll stay out there as long as he can.

"THE TONGUE SAYS LONELINESS, ANGER, GRIEF,
BUT DOES NOT FEEL THEM."

—Jane Hirshfield, "The Tongue Says Loneliness"

Not so.
Stammering, the tongue
pressed to the teeth says *Terror,*

whistles, bird-like, with delight.
The tongue that shapes the windpipe's
warm air into midnight

shushings of mother and child
is instrument of the prophet's
curse and blessing.

The tongue tastes vinegar and milk,
oranges and cinnamon,
the salty sweets of another's lips.

AT FIRST

I wanted to come back.
I was just beginning to get the hang of things.
Love, for instance.

I'd hardly come to know who I was.
I was something, wasn't I?
It would be a mistake to think of me now

as vapor or odorless spirit,
as someone else's invention. Nothing
prepared me for this . . . one veil lifts, then another.

So many times I'd been told
I was beautiful. That I was *loved.*
In the end it was relief

to find out that we belong to love.
When the stranger who found me that night
laid his coat over my body, I wanted

to weep, but couldn't, of course.
I am beyond harm now.
I've grown accustomed to the faint

yet curiously persistent singing here.
I like to think it is the unborn practicing,
waiting for time to begin.

DEAREST WILLIAM,

I urge you not to delay.
Nothing more can be done for him now.
Do you think a man has two lifetimes
to see his father? You've whittled away
enough time keeping to yourself.
Besides, we two never did say good-bye.

Leaves sheer from the maples,
alizarin-crimson, umber, the gold-orange
the trees on this street always favored.
All my life I wanted to paint
what I was paying attention to.
Remember when I tried to paint you?
I keep to this work of nursing others.

I know he was a harsh man, William.
Always had a burr in his throat
when he spoke to you, but I can't forget
how he saved my father's life that winter
he pulled him out of Jacob's Pond
at the risk of his own. A *damn fool*,
he called my father, for stepping out
on the ice after snowmelt.

Don't wait until the last breath plows
his lungs dry. I've seen it too many times.
You'll be glad for a flicker of recognition
when words no longer matter.

With affection,

Kathryn

THE MAN IN THE NEXT PEW

lets go of his cane and holds
with both hands the pew ahead of him.
Now and then he dips down, shaking,
pulls himself back up. Stands still
as he can while the Gospel's read.
Today the *Parable of the Sower*.
Pastor says he thinks it's less
about what kind of soil we are—
rocky, weed-choked, good—
and more about God's extravagance.
Afraid my neighbor will fall
I keep my eye on his resolve.
Love's grip gives and sways.

I'LL NEVER KNOW

When you roared
out of your darkest places
like a bear from the wild,
I did not tell.

Crow, like the heart,
is a master of silence,
even in sunlight carries
a thousand grains of darkness.

The last time
you asked me to hold you
I did not, for fear
you'd hold me back.

Even in happiness
we trembled with exhaustion.

MOSS

makes of this rock a small mountain,
         steep slopes, ledges and cliffs
cushioned in greens the eye
                  sinks into: up close,

feather moss, rootless primitive whose soft, ever-
         reaching fronds are really
needles on a stem. To live at the level
                  of moss! To walk

in its low-lying forests listening
         to the soft, dry pattering down of spores,
insect dust, snippets of vegetation.
                  Close to ground

or scaling walls, moss holds tight, is good
         in crisis; can do without, gone from green
to gold to friable brown until you think
                  it's dead.

One day it springs up again, grows expansive
         beneath rain's broad touch,
moss finger-soothing, forgiving
                  underfoot.

MORNING GLORIES

To think I planted
      what seemed heavenly, a drift
         of azure silks,

now frost-stung to darkest ultramarine.
      They hold themselves up
         though the petals

shrivel and furl back, bruised, the way the skin
      on your hands, after chemo,
         peels untidily

to waves of hot pain.
      But what a surge of bloom to come: hundreds
         of tightly whorled buds

still rise above the deck rail
      like sea shells glazed with celadon,
         green incandescences

that seem to say,
      What else can the world do
         but consume us?

No good trying to compare your going
      to this near gorgeous ruin.
         Let these blooms

be small Victrolas swelling into song,
      some sentimental tune
         about the steadiness

of someone's love,
      and this tangle of vines
         unwind—one long

unburdened thought
      taking shape as gesture,
         a word finally said.

II

CONSIDER

On Roger van der Weyden's painting
The Escorial Deposition, c. 1435

that beauty might be dangerous,
that you might lose yourself in Magdalene's
curved flesh, dance of grief so perfectly composed
you rock and sway.

A crowd has gathered
and where there's an inch to spare
gold light shines at their backs. Tenderly,
Joseph of Arimathea carries Christ down from the cross.
He steps across the Virgin's robe
so as not to disturb that river of tortuous
indigo folds—

       (like the room you dared not enter,
       the sound of someone's grief holding you back).

       It's a story of hands
(a study in voicelessness), hands lifting, twined, touching
so lightly you'd cry out for this, hands repeating
the way the name of a lost one echoes
against a canyon wall.
       One arm hangs down,
plumb line that holds the world steady

       (around earth's axis, the bedside vase's
       single tilting stem)

even as Mary falls behind him, the cupped fingers
of her limp arm a bowl from which
nothing spills.

If the sheer pleasure of seeing leads us
not closer but farther away, or not close enough,
what have we done?
       Outside

the cardinal swims though the trees
       like the scarlet movement of stocking, cloak
and sleeve, like the rivulets of blood
in their refusal to be astonishing;
eyes wander the crowd
until they come to rest, exhausted,
as after a bout of weeping.
       And begin again.

KINDNESS

Never
glamorous,
seldom forgotten.

Modest in proportion—
kindling
slow, quiet.

Touch without grip.

STILL LIFE: NEARLY RECLINING WOMAN, SETTEE AND LEANING AXE

Sitting beside the handle of this axe,
it's not the thwack and splitting
open of pine log and linden
I think of.

No, I'm thinking about the way
one thing leans into another, wood
to cushion, cushion to skin,
skin to skin.

Though I'm tempted
to consider memory as the trace of one thing
held inside another, slide of a hand up and down
that swung length of hickory
smoothed to the cleanness of bone,
I think mostly of rest,

the good heft of a thing being itself on earth,
green field and four small trees,
apple, pear, two ash.

For Hours

          For hours it seems it will rain,
the sky dampening the nasturtiums' scarlet blooms
                    to dull flares on the porch,
then sun again, brilliant—
                    gleam culling night
from the deep shade of hosta and sugar maple, the desire
          for sleep. Then it's dark again, then light, back
                    and forth. Each round note of the mourning
          dove
     is a sigh, held and let go, held, let go,
  as if from a house far away and you say,
                    I know this song, I knew it once.

          The day draws out like a long conversation
                    between two unlikely selves
quietly astonished; one thought turns easily toward another,
          anything might be said now,
                    no shame, fear suspended
like the rain, notes rising and falling over the white chair,
          over the ruffled blooms and black earth, *Yes,*
                    and *Yes.*

It does not matter if it rains now.
You live, longing
          for this never to end.

FUGUE OF THE LONG TRACE

At last, he invented a map made of music.
That morning, he placed on his desk a white chrysanthemum,
and, detached as the blue feather he found on his lawn,
began to beat time and hum the minimal tune.

So mysterious was the sound released through his open window,
the neighbors stopped what they were doing. Turning
their faces toward the yard where gold and white chrysanthemums
bloomed in profusion each fall, they forgot where they were.

(It was inevitable, the report of metal, underground
a shattering of bulbs so that earthworms, once thought
to be deaf, rolled their soft, ringed bodies against the dark.)
In the singing he was like a moth against an avalanche, the terrible

silences that go round and round, until he found an unexpected change of key,
island of vertigo. When they found him, chrysanthemum
crushed in his palm, a few petals lay arranged like long white notes
on the cabbage rose carpet, revealing a set of harmonies previously unknown.

That evening a lapis-winged bird was seen hovering near his window:
it repeated through the night a song of such liquidity that those who heard it
were filled with a longing like the thirst of angels in a waterless heaven.
Ornithologists rejoiced at the possible sighting of a new species

conjectured to have lost its way traveling from one remote
latitude to another, but the song proved unrecordable.
For weeks the neighbors slept restlessly while the local river
rose to its highest levels in human history.

FANTAZIA "UPON ONE NOTE"

—Henry Purcell (1659 - 1695)

One note, a constancy
tempered wood and gut insist
on singing, like one word repeated almost endlessly,

this C other voices talk back and forth across,
fantastic as the elegant writhe
of flames about a burning stick.

Composer's trick, this C, airy sleight of hand?
Or simply one note to play
for the friend who could hardly play the viol?

We step away from, step toward it, *glissando*–
Oh, we want to be steady, we do.
We need this C, this middle ground

offered like a determined view of the world from one window.

WITHOUT SAYING A WORD

I left the river and walked to the high meadow
to hear the wind instead of water.

The hot air tuned the crickets to a single pitch.
There was so much to consider, the tangle
of yellow coltsfoot and purple vetch, kingbird
and swallow wreathing the thickets,
all flicker and intention.

I sat down among the grasses to rest.
I turned my head to see what I thought
must be the swirl and rustle of a skirt, my sister
bending down to gather more flowers
and lay her hand on warm earth.

The sun burned relentlessly.
Wind swept over the island.
I left the grasses without saying a word.
Was it only the heart's reluctance to follow?

Something saw me at noonlight in the high meadow.
I might have heard its cry of astonishment
had it not been for the constancy of the wind.

HONESTY

A sip
of its cordial—
bitter or bracing—
sends one fleeing,
calls another home.

Can be diluted.
Refused.
Taken neat.

Soul's tonic
depending on
who's pouring,
the cup
it's poured into.

RUMORS

All night the bee that's clung
      to the sunflower, dark as
           coffee, waits for the sun

to warm its stilled apparatus,
      one leg ticking like the hand of a tiny clock
           that can't get started.

See how the morning glories,
      like closed umbrellas glazed
           with rain, open in the cool air

to cobalt cups of heaven,
      or the *idea* of heaven, gone
           by noon. The wood thrush

I've never seen repeats
      last night's song, trill and lick
           spilling from the flute of its throat

as if it knows a rigorous joy,
      as if the world's consolable.
           Blue sky, clear and widened

like a mind that's looked into itself and beyond,
      is this what we fear, or long for?
           Caught

in the undertow of the linden's shade,
      rumors of something sweet and light
           and never forgotten.

THE MAN AND WOMAN RAKING LEAVES DO NOT SPEAK
OF FABULOUS THINGS

Bit by bit, they gather whatever gold trappings the trees
      have shed, pulling leaves from the tines
like pieces of lint. They bend over their voices, holding them
      close to earth, hushed as a murmur
of bees. She imagines a country where the sound of
      the late, rasping cricket under the lilac
might cover the footsteps of a man fleeing. Wearied
      of her inwardness

her husband imagines a pull so strong
      it makes leaves lifted by the wind spiral back
and go nowhere. Is this sighing over scraped ground
      how much he desires of her that he cannot have,
or knowledge of how large a world he could hold?
      In another country, a man imagines
a night darker than coffee, as fragrant:
      this he could pass through

to the other side. He tastes iron in his mouth (his own blood
      or fear, heart pounding so loudly
it could pull the moon into place?). Under the trees by the feeder
      the man and woman laugh at the blue jay's
outrage: *possess, possess, possess.*
      Soon they will lie down in the house together.
There are no borders, she thinks, only states
      of feeling, boredom, fear, elation,

whatever love is (these endless leaves
      exhaust her, she who has chosen
to live at the edge of a woods). She would like to stop
      everything and listen: *Whoever lies down in the grass*
will gain the earth's ear. The bamboo and metal tines
      click like beetles that could live in a desert,
anywhere. A world away, the man running for his life
      tries not to imagine daylight, blue

that is the memory of something else,
   song about the sky his grandmother sang,
cup of goat's milk, not this yard where the leaves are falling
   and the sky is blue. *The world is so large,*
the man lifting leaves would like to say to his wife.
   He loves this day, the trees, the black
arc of hair against her cheek, the cricket, the grand
   sweep of their rakes.

SOMETIMES I WISH THE RAIN

could wash my impatience away,
my hardness of heart rinsed like grit
from the blackberry bush by the road,

the soaked boughs of the sassafras
bobbing in the day-after wind
like waves in a lake, a spray of droplets
suddenly shaken down.

I could stand in the field surrounded
by such luxury and feel for a moment lighter
as if I'd forgiven one thing, *one*.

WAS IT ONLY THE WIND

or a subtler provocation
in the tall cage of the miscanthus
that distracted the catbird
and wren? To the one

who worked the garden
it registered as a delicate
attenuation of feeling, a sense
of something pulled back

into the world from archaic
slumber, spirit matter
left in the rock's crevices
hollowed out sea ages ago

and now come to light
on the skin of her wrist.
She knelt in the dirt
like the old woman

who can weigh earth's desires
called up from the dark-
ness of words before
they are spoken.

PATIENCE

Patience
properly
applied
exacts
a toll—
immediate—
that might
in time
unloose
the roar
of the beautiful.

We stood there for hours, waiting
for a summoning. How quickly the seasons passed
on the steep bank of the sky, full moon, dark hills,
a concordance of swallows from no place
we'd been on earth.

So many losses to attend and our bodies light now—
Was it early or late? The beginning, or the end?
No fires in the sky nor angels descending, their silent
wide open mouths singing with the force of an untamable joy.
It was a dream, and not a dream: in the distance, centuries of armies
passed without a sound on plains flocked with rubble.
To the east, a city glowed and hummed
with the interiority of bees.

Soon it would be evening again; there would be a child crying.
Still, the shadows did not lengthen.
We walked back down into the green sward of the valley,
the small weight in our hearts lessened,
our voices quieter now.

III

FROM

From a crease of time
so brief it was nearly missed
I woke. Became window and veil,

green ardor of leaves, snowdrift, swimming cell,
hermitage and high wire act. Claimed
as my own, clenched fingers, lips

tasting lips, beads of sweat.
I sang a psalm of praise for apples and bread,
elegy for a dark-spotted lung. Accuser

and the one forgiven, I was reliquary, clay vessel,
bowl emptied and filled, emptied and filled.
Tinderbox of love.

she fell into a clump of switch grass—*damn!*
the first expletive was born. She stood up slowly,
expecting to hear the usual vegetal and winged
murmurs of the night, not the popping sound
of stones sprouted by frost.

Her feet were cold, to say nothing of the rest of her.
Strangely thrilled, she wondered how anyone
could live in such a place. She'd need more
than a blanket of grass to keep her warm, she'd need
the skin of an animal she'd have to kill . . .

Arms wrapped about herself, sighing,
ah, the warm length of the man's torso and limbs.
Now the sound of grumbling, or was it lovemaking?
And that orange glow, the uncertain flickerings of fire?
Perhaps it wasn't so different here after all

though who would leave everything they'd been given for this?
She felt a rich stirring of the mind, hunger for the cradle
of a language as yet unborn—destiny and free will,
gravity and dark matter, longsuffering—
so much for their later claims

that it wasn't in her nature to think this way.
Wasn't she creating as she went along
like the one who'd brought all this into being,
who spoke to them daily? She loved
these questions, even if she was freezing.

WHY WE DO NOT CUT THE MEADOW DOWN

It establishes itself like the sea.
We ride its swells.
Two kinds of dragonfly, cobalt and crimson,
a pair of catbirds, orioles skim the tops of the grasses,
insect glints, multitudes unnamed.

Once it was an orchard, a woods,
before that a real sea that left us a lake.
Today the dry meadow is all fire and pulse—
hot sputter of crickets, bees cruising the nightshade,
the wings of a small white butterfly dipping at *this* and *that*,
yes and *yes* above the grasses where light assembles.

The meadow admits stray saplings, cottonwood and ash.
Opens to rain like a body full of desire.
The fringed flags of the grasses take note of
the least wind: when you think it's still
a cloud of pollen swells and lifts.

The meadow does not mistake the seed—
scutcheoned, tasseled or winged—for anything else.
Whatever comes into the meadow, earthworm, black beetle, ant,
feels the long fall of sunlight on its back
before it descends.

THE MIDNIGHT HOUSE

My mother made me cups of tea those nights
I couldn't breathe. We'd sit in the stairwell landing
in our nightgowns, sipping the bitter drink.

Breathe the steam, it'll open your lungs, she'd say.
Can you die of this? I'd ask, gasping.
Of course not, she'd answer, and I believed.

Sometimes she'd have to call the doctor.
He came with his black bag of tricks, syringe
of adrenalin to set my small heart thumping.

Years later she grew ill and difficult and sometimes mean.
One day she pushed her wheelchair into the road
then lifted her hands from the wheel

as to free herself. *Damn you,*
I muttered under my breath, chasing her,
my heart, now larger, beating hard. My husband

never understood why I cared for her. I loved her
for that medicine we shared in the dark, her company
that kept me there, while all the others slept.

HALF-LOST

Hypnotic, the toss
and leap of pillowcases, clothes—
half-lost socks, shirts and jeans
spinning over and under
each other, dark

and light mixed,
though who'd bark at me now—
our mother's ghost—

mother who taught us
to iron pillowcases, sheets.
Crease with steam the sleeves
of our blouses until
the fabric shone.

She'd grieve for me now,
for the house I lost. The home.

I reach into the mound,
deliberate as a surgeon's hand
plunging into the body's
heat—heart waiting
to be fixed, pulsing lung—
warmer than the skin of anyone
who's worn these clothes,
of anyone I've loved.

> . . . *he drew his creature's understanding into*
> *his side by the same wound; and there he revealed*
> *a fair and delectable place for all mankind* . . .

—Julian of Norwich (1342–1416)
from *Revelations of Divine Love*, 10th *Revelation*

If the wind is servant to fire and grass,
what of seed, spore, calcium, dust?
Nothing conceived in darkness forgets.
My brother is studying the nature of madness.

What of seed, spore, calcium, dust:
are they singing against silence or in praise of it?
My brother is studying the nature of madness
because things that are lost have many names.

Are they singing against silence or in praise of it?
All these years, he wanted to feel rapture, once.
Because things that die quietly have many names,
how do we know a self exists?

All these years, he wanted to feel rapture.
When we come to this earth, what do we know?
How do we know a self exists?
Julian sees *a fair and delectable place for all mankind.*

When we come to this earth, what do we know?
That there is water, then blood; there are fingers, then a song,
a fair and delectable place for all mankind?
Touch the inside of a wound:

water and blood; fingers, then a song.
Nothing conceived in darkness forgets
touching the inside of a wound,
that wind is servant to fire and grass.

WAKING ON THE ANNIVERSARY OF YOUR DEATH

–for my sister

3:33 a.m., I'm up and about, night black as a bruised nail.
Above the crickets' throbbing, wind roves through the trees
like a rough hand through hair.
                              No one here,
or so it seems.
I've been reading the letters of the living and the dead,
what I didn't want to know about, your narcotic bliss
before the body's letting down.
        To die without dying, you wrote.

Cloud cover low through which
a few stars gleam faintly, equation of light
and dark that won't balance.

Twenty six years later I still don't know what to say
here in this five-fold darkness
filled with the sound of wind
pilfering the leaves.

4:00 a.m. under the stars' soft shine.
Nothing to do but turn in.
If the light bends down, if . . .
love us, Lord.

the field's excess of light, the day floating on itself as in a dream.
But it isn't a dream, the wound songs of the house finch,
the sun hammering the grasses' bronze tips.
We had gathered about your bed

like a boat we tried to push off stony ground.
We wanted to help: we believed in the buoyancy of that water.
You held onto the ruins instead of our hands.
What did we know of how it is to look back at one's life?

A bee swings from the nightshade.
Ants carry their burden up the post of the shed unmoved by song.
The grasses bend under the weight of so much light.
And the balm of the wind: from the woods the singing of leaves.
Or is it the sound of water flowing?

I wonder if we'd recognize each other now?
It's not the graying but the way gravity
takes hold of the face's finest parts. This morning
it seems this pale wash of sun on my kitchen walls
barely made it through the winter.
I expect you've been happy these years;
that was your great gift, to gather goodness around you.

I never moved to the big city to teach piano.
Still play for the choir, never lost my love for Bach.
Not a sad life, though more modest than I'd imagined.
I've had to find the largeness of the world
in small things. There's a time we think we have several lives
ahead of us, never one choice cancelling another.
It's true I regret not choosing you.
I told myself I was afraid I couldn't be myself in your world.

I've a son, yes, a professor at the nearby university.
He's a kind man, thoughtful, as you'd expect,
soon to be married. No, I never married.
I suppose all this surprises you. I think about the nature
of this world and the next; if it's meant to be, it will be.
I look into the night sky or the depths of my old maple
for comfort from a god who never seemed to rest a hand on *my* head.
More like someone who's watching me from a distance
and knows I'll get there.

Those summer nights on the hill
we lay on the grass and talked about space and time,
the mystery of our being here at all, let alone with each other.
Now that so much time has passed, my heart's
no longer weighed down by the anchor of longing.
I'd like to know how you are, that you are well
and your life's come to some good.

My sister who loves all things Egyptian
once asked me what I would take into the next world.
I think it would be the memory of those nights,
the darkness and our words. I'd compare
what we thought with what is.

IF I DECIDE TO PRAY AGAIN IT WON'T BE WORDS
STRUNG IN A LINE

I'm going to pray with my whole body.
        I don't mean snake-handling
sanctifications in a wood's hollow nor torso rolling,
        arm waving hollering on a carpeted aisle.
          No, God of dark matter

and everything in-between, I'm going to concentrate
        every particle of my being,
each neuron strumming molecule, each cell
        pitching and sliding beneath the cloak
        of my skin

in a rib-tingling, knuckles humming, heart tilting
        quiet fire in the throat prayer:
make of this flesh-in-air a window seen through
        to that countenance of love shining
        its ordinary face.

NOCTURNE

I step from our bed
to the open window. Through layers of mist
the frayed sound of insects streams,

earth inventing herself again.
I close my eyes, wish I could pour
myself into that singing

and turn into the creature
I've never been, decisive as the heron
yet supple as a green leaf

spilling rain, fierce
as the she-bear in spring.
How much of memory am I willing

to let go? By morning, I think,
it will be gone, the lush pull of this night
beyond everything I've chosen.

WE TURN OUT OF THE WIND,

two wool coated friends happy
with talk about books and the lunacy
of families—your 96-year-old mother,
Russian-speaking, demented, insists
you find your brother's unmarked grave
in Siberia. What mother doesn't want
to know where her child
is buried?
       In another century
we'd be pushing our wheelbarrow of potatoes
in a field raked by November's fading light,
two women who, though weary, talk heartily,
as if they'd lifted suffering out of the earth
and turned it into something good to eat.

I WANTED TO VISIT THE PLANET REVOLVING
AROUND TWO SUNS

Astronomers say they've now found a planet
that orbits two suns a mere thousand trillion
miles from here. —Richard Harris, NPR, Sept. 15, 2011

They said nothing could live there.
I didn't care: I closed my eyes and left.

Some days the orange disc
of the sun I named Lucano
slipped below the horizon
before the gorgeous, scarlet Leonora.

On others she plunged first
as if singing a last aria to the lover
she didn't know was chasing her. I loved best
the days they sank together in a wild blaze.

Round and round we turned, they
about each other, I, on my planet, about them,
a threesome's strange love affair that worked.

If it was cold sitting on my campstool
in that desert of rock and gases, knapsack
of provisions at my feet, fur coat wrapped around me,
I was hardly ever unhappy,
only myself to feed and nowhere
the voice of argument.

I began to miss Earth's fumy vapors
igniting the skies over her parking lots and plazas.
Even her moon, cool, unflappable.
I came home.

Some days now, it's not so bad,
voices rising and falling about me—
gossip and politics, talk about my barking dog.
I have an opera to finish.
A fur coat to mend.

STILL LIFE

> *What talks we had. One evening we discussed*
> *Mormonism, the medieval ramparts of Aigues Mortes,*
> *and the pronunciation of ancient Greek.*
>
> *–1911 T. Griffith Taylor*
> (From *Still Life: inside the Antarctic huts of Scott*
> *and Shackleton.* Photography by Jane Ussher)

A pair of gloves, creased, oil-grimed, holds
the shape of fingers that kept what heat
they could until the stove, blubber-stoked,
smoked the walls with stink and shadows.

Tins of beef paste and tobacco. Rusted chains.

Troglodytes, they called themselves
and yet sang Church of England hymns
before Sunday dinners of mutton and ham,
their carcasses still strung up, a century frozen.

Incubator. Chronometer. Algae nets, flasks.

Grubby striped pajamas hang on the wall
ready to be slipped over shoulders and hips
as on those nights they lay here talking
history warmed by the heat of their words.

THE WIND REFUSES TO FORGET

> Only a severed finger was returned
> from each of the bodies.
>
> —from an NPR hourly news report,
> March 2008

The one bruised
by hammer and rock
knew also the coolness of stone

rolled in the pocket, traced a name
in dust, hollow of a lover's throat.
Steered lever, joystick,

shovel, wheel, bullet and blade,
was part of a hand that wanted to strike
and did, a time or two.

In the great cities
hailed the cab. Pointed, *This way.*
Held aloft, told the wind's direction.

THIS DAY

—in memory of George C. Utech,
1931-2009

A boy sits in the barn in the dark,
the lantern he's lugged into the night laid just so, to milk by.
He rests his head against her warm, pungent side.
Up, down, his fingers knead and pull.
The white streams rush out like all that's good in the world.

Iowa, 1944. He's blessed by parentage
and place and who he is. His mind's eye spirals up
past hawkweed, fox in the henhouse, his mother's
clear blue eyes; dreams galaxies and God. Soon
he'll walk back to the house to drink the one cup of coffee
allowed, then it's off to school.

Just before dawn, he nears the house
where a breeze lifts the maple's black leaves.
He feels a quiet thrilling in the midst of a generous calm
he'll carry all his life. This day—its dark, its voices
calling from the kitchen door, open, lit—begins again.

NIGHTS, ALONE, FROM HER CHAIR

You'd think it slovenly, how nights
I sleep in this chair, your father's army blanket
thrown over me, so I can keep my eye on the yard
and hill beyond. This view may be the last thing I own.
I like to wake early, let my thoughts settle
before the sky goes milky blue and sunlight
turns the snowy curve of that hill into strands
of saffron melting in a broth.

I've finally learned how to *be* in this house,
surrounded by sounds that have deepened with time,
those floorboards at the foot of the stairs
that only take a change of weather to speak.
There's comfort to be drawn from what you expect
though I admit I've startled at the breaking
loose of ice from the roof sudden as a cliff face
tumbling out of itself. That's what I am now,
a small force of nature, almost spent.

So much desire in the beginning.
Would you believe I was a flower once?
All that unfolding. I was crazy for your father.
We found the cracks in each other, channels
of darkness that only widen with use. That's
love, imperfect, squaring with the truth,
deciding how to come to terms with it.

Now I'll make a cup of tea and wash
a few things. Maybe gather up this old blanket
and haul it out to the porch railing,
let the pure cold of this January day rinse it clean.

A GREAT TENDERNESS

Even now it exists: the room without me, the blue bowl filled
       with dried gingko leaves,
and the deep sill in which afternoon light pools
when I cannot return by nostalgia
or touch.

To think I should have been here at all. And the small maple
at the corner of the house that held moonlight those nights
I could not sleep—surely *it* was real?
And the body beside mine, our plummeting and
       rising together,
what time permitted us to do.

There must have been fields
of those flowers. Blue.
Lupine and flax. Cornflower blue.
Something *seen*, head turned toward the window:
lace curtain, white shade, the light too much.
How many layers to go through? Slight milkiness
of cataracts, water rushing over rock?
Every line erased, fine yellow skin smoothed
over the high forehead and aquiline nose.
All agitation ceased now, mask of a mask, radiant
over interior ruin. The body a husk and God
in the eyes gone. Relic of blue glass. Mouth
of awe open: O. The roaring of wind with no sound.

ST. MARGARETE'S ISLAND, ST. LAWRENCE RIVER

—for my sons

We slip into the canoe, the moon
cloud-banked. My sons dip their paddles
 into molten black glass. I let my fingers
trail in water a few inches and no deeper.
 Here and there an island's lamp burns
like a mind against its own darkness.
 We might not be real but for the murmur
of our voices, the unhurried drip of river
 back into river, drinking itself. We glide,
cradled in the grip of slow black swells.
 Tenderly they steer me home.

MORNINGS WHEN I DRINK MY COFFEE

I taste the sweetness of God.
Ridiculous, you say, my spoon ringing on china
the praises of coffee, good coffee, strong coffee, bitterness
laced with cream bathing the night-thickened throat,
heart and mind quickened.

So what if torturer and accomplice drink coffee at their table.
And the liar, the cheat, the gossip.
Gather round surgeons, lovers, poets, garbage-pickers!
And the midnight crew at the docking station
where everything enters this world.

All day I long for the taste of that first sip.
Why is it never enough? Still, is it not good,
the pouring and emptying, the receiving and letting go
from the cup which warms the hands held to it?
Let me be buried with the ancients in their earth mounds,
my coffee-making apparatus laid alongside me
and this cup over which our words passed.

If there is a heaven surely its angels
are tending great urns of coffee, taking turns
grinding, brewing, pouring. We'll sit at a shining table
telling our story, everything we were afraid to say.
Laugh at our foolishness, forgive a thing or two,
the earthly aroma of coffee rising
around us, awakened at last.

CARDIOLOGY

Just keep puttering along, my dear,
the doctor says, like some vintage car
dusting a country road, though my heart's
by far the youngest in this office and lively
in its leaping. Sparks in all the wrong places.

The summer before I left my marriage, I practiced
going farther but not faster, not if I wanted
to stay alive. Emily says *Hope is the thing*
with feathers, but I'll take moving lightly
over asphalt, small spring in my step, heart
taking its time trying not to fly.

RUE

I'm miserable, you're missed, if ever you
existed. That more than one spectacular kiss. Mon dieu,
self-pity's the worst guest when one is one, not two.

Does thinking, day and night, as I think of you
make one love one's own life less? Let's say love grew
then diminished, the way twin stars, revolving, brew

themselves to death. Our love, true,
was imperfect, though I swear past, present, fu-
ture (a trick?) dissolved in it. A canoe's

quivering dance on still water. What now in lieu
of love that poured so many cups of tea? Made stew,
your favorite, on winter nights. Grounded like emus

I thought we were, by love, not gravity, until we flew
apart. Later I wondered, had I only imagined you?
Hard to put one's faith in a longer, larger view

of Love: desire doesn't ring a bell but shudders through
the body. Is there more than one of you?
Should I go hunting, madly woo

lips, belly, teeth and tongue? Anyone's? Undo
this grief, dearest one. Say that all along you knew
I was coming. Fantastic me, fantastic you. This blue

that haunts me is not the tender hue
of spring forget-me-nots we picked but dark—stop.
Or this will be the end of me. Of lovely, improbable you.

Keeping House

Leave behind a marriage, a house, and just
when you think you're done with all those bits
of yesterday you wept for, there's still dust,
dust on this tabletop your fingers trace

a smooth, winding river across: flakes
of skin and broken hair, sheddings of paper,
collars, cuffs, gathered into the soft folds
of your cloth. What they say about

wiping the slate clean—can't be done.
If you think sorrow's a stranger here, think again.
And love, well love, come on in, and for heaven's sake
shake from your feet the dust you'll bring.

IV

THE INVISIBLE STENOGRAPHER RECORDS
THE EVIDENCE SHE'S BEEN GIVEN

Sitting at her desk with a pack of the Marlboros
she's tried to give up a million times,
she can find a shorthand for almost everything,
the number of casualties left unreported,
the stentorious sigh of a cow after labor,
rootlets fingering the savage
sweetness of the dirt.

She likes the comfort of these side-zip twills
with a touch of lycra, but she's worn it all: shirtwaists
underwired by girdle and bra, empire-waisted gowns,
deerskin tunics, the hair shirts of saints, pleated chiton
draped just below the low slung beauty
of her left breast.

From the outset she was the obsessive type,
maker of lists: dates, births and deaths, diagnoses,
times of arrival and departure, the amassing of coins, weapons
and works of art, portions of letters, speeches and grocery lists,
though soon it was statements of motivation, speculations
on the nature of the original crime,
the 33 million names for God.

At times she can be heard humming in the background,
taking a break to clip her nails, for this is the work
of hands and she must keep them neat,
which might explain the occasional missing fact,
the life left out all together.

There are moments she stops to ask,
Aren't we all minions of starlight?
Which has traveled farthest from where it began, the ant
*   or a speck of dust?*
How much thinking is a thought?

Who knows, in another life she might come back
wearing a raiment of snow,
able to walk in the least hint of radiance.

THE INVISIBLE STENOGRAPHER'S PENCIL
FALLS INTO THE GREAT ABYSS

It's happened before,
hammer and chisel, stylus, quill—
but this one she loved, how it drew
from her fingertips loops and scrawls,
spirited, expansive, unswerving.

Lovers at ease with their newly
found touch, she and her pencil, recorded
the discovery of galaxies, rare northern mosses,
the displacement of air by a soprano's high C
relative to the weight of the soul.

They nearly lifted the unbearable from our sight:
the image of his mother's face floating behind the murderer's eye
the moment before he struck;
the suicide's last words:
I can't bear the darkness now.

She could write volumes
on the history of the shadow and its uses:
Notes on the Shape of Light's Absence
as Evidence of the Object Itself.

Easy enough to be swept into the void herself.
She reaches for another stick of graphite,
soft, lustrous, flowing like a river of carbon
from the core of the earth.

THE INVISIBLE STENOGRAPHER PONDERS HER ORIGINS

Some days she would like to cry out:
Where did I come from, O great one?

Have I mother and father,
or am I orphan of ocean and air?
Did I lie alongside the flatworm and sea cucumber,
the cuttlefish and giant sea snail at the beginning of days?
Was the space between stars my first cradle?

She licks the tip of her pencil and sighs.
Without complaint, she's sung the centuries down—
chronicled flood and war, cease fire and plague,
arrivals, departures, siroccos, monsoons, cataclysms and rifts.
Where among these is the record of *her* birth?

Or did she simply appear at the mouth of fog and mist?
Rise from decay, a bluebottle fly from a stinking heap?

Did cherubim and seraphim cease
their chanting at the moment she appeared?
Did she fly, fully formed, from the sparks of their wings
or was she left at their feet by anxious souls?

Where is the angel she requested to sit at her side,
instead of this squawking parrot in the back room
she must cover night and day?

THE INVISIBLE STENOGRAPHER CONSIDERS
THE EXISTENCE OF ANGELS

In all these years she's not seen one,
though she doesn't know how she gets her work done,
a miracle really. Sparrow hawk, house finch,

hummingbird—they might be disguises,
but wouldn't she know the filmy
void of a wing on her arm,

the heat of radiant breath in her ear?
God knows how many centuries of sightings
she's reported on desert highways,

boats, the back of cars. Better
to ignore that swarm of voices itinerant
as the wind. It's not prophecy

or poetry she's after, but someone
who'll guide her wrist, bring her a glass
of cool water at the end of the day.

.

WHILE TAKING A NAP, THE INVISIBLE STENOGRAPHER DREAMS SHE CAN PLAY THE VIOLIN

Cithern, lyre, lute, viola d'amore—
all her life she's dreamt of playing
something she can stroke
and pluck, pass her hand over.

She lifts her bow in the empty hall,
dark but for the circle of light she stands in.
Notes spiral out, as if from her throat,
then descend in a near ruinous scale, quiver
and soar until she's lifted out of herself, this world.

She's learned this piece by heart.
Now she invents as she goes, swaying
at the knees, *glissando,*
accelerando,
piz-zi-cato–

She wonders if there's someone in the darkness
listening to the jazz riff she's arrived at,
sweet licks of sound, hot, sexy,
a little sad, the voice
she didn't know she had.

THE INVISIBLE STENOGRAPHER RENTS A SMALL MOTORBOAT

She pulls the choke, after a sputter or two
cruises out between the islands. She loves
the fierce slap of this cold northern river
on aluminum hull.

Out where no one can hear her, she shouts at the gulls,
Let the historians argue behind closed doors!
Let the dead languages languish!
Let the typists record the death tolls
and transactions in gold!

She cuts the motor and drifts. Loose jacketed,
pole in hand, hair tucked into a baseball cap,
she could be a man.

Balanced between water and sky,
she could be anyone.

THE INVISIBLE STENOGRAPHER REDISCOVERS THE WHEEL

Seems like only yesterday,
the log roller, then potter's wheel
and Sumerian chariot, fixed axle and spoke,
tires leather and metal (not until 1888 Dunlap's pneumatic tire),
and don't forget the water wheel, pulley, windlass and clock,
all the possibilities and problems
of continuous motion.

Is it boredom or the cloudless blue sky that sends her
five stories down from the rooms where she writes these days
to the 3-speed red bicycle someone's left to rust in the alley?
She hops on expecting to tip but it's as if
she's always known how the pedal's resistance
melts between two walls of air.

She wonders how fine a line she could trace
between what's true and false, the self and the other, the yin
and yang of it all. This point she's balancing on
could be the present turning into the past, all the possible
lines of the future fanning out before her.
She rides no hands, a wheelie, lifted
out of time and space.

Prayer wheel, mandala, untouchable, unnamable nothing,
she sings, pedaling faster and faster until breathless.
Legs aching, she thinks she may be human after all.
Red streamers shoot like flames
from her wrists. From a distance
she's nothing more than a furious scribbling
across the face of the earth.

THE INVISIBLE STENOGRAPHER CONSIDERS
THE METAPHYSICAL LIFE,

a return to the classrooms of thought.
Who can say if she really exists?
What can the mind know independent of itself?

Time to put aside the stuff of the world,
relics, bones, catalogues of inventions,
their manuals for operation
and repair,

every stone etched rune,
coroners' reports, ink's travail on the page,
letters arriving to say *how the journey
was hard, the winters long.*

What of the sinopia drawings
hidden beneath the paintings of her beloved
Italian Master, under torment and bliss, lapis, burnt sienna and gold,
brush strokes revealing the artist's *pentimenti,*
his very thoughts?

A few lines of red earth
holding up the whole gorgeous mess.

after a day of indexing war crimes,
the Invisible Stenographer reconsiders her vocation.
She likes the idea of "an occult relation
between man and the vegetable,"
its potential harmonizing influence.
And hasn't she always been a "transparent eyeball"?
She prides herself on sticking close to the facts,
the precise wording of the coroner's reports.

 "I am nothing. I see all" could be her mantra.
Today she'd like to lie on the slope of a shaded leaf,
eyes closed, and enter the hallowed cave of the mighty baobab.
Be an acre of wheat undone by the wind.

because there's always another book,
the codex as yet undiscovered. Even the forgeries,
leather bound and crumbling, caked
by some idiot with gesso and mud, are real.
Inside, the skin of an animal tattooed
with the lost discourse they've been looking for,
mathematical proof of divine intent,
runes, ant trails, quarkian paths.

THE INVISIBLE STENOGRAPHER TRIES NOT TO LOOK IN THE MIRROR

What would she see—
      transparency
of oxygen, or eyes smudged with kohl?

Head-binding wimple.
      Sky blue burkha.
Iron brank tearing into the tongue
which said too much.

A cat mask, candle-lit, trimmed
with gold sequins and feathers
     the color of a bishop's robe.

Hematite lips, lips drawn in rose madder;
cheeks ash streaked; tattooed;
    white powdered, porcelain smooth.

    A single pearl drop earring
dangling above a creamy ruff
    of Belgian lace
stained from centuries of use.

Is everything she sees
who she is?
   Why not a coiled forest of dreadlocks,
or the shapeliness of a head
shaved to the cool shine of the moon?

Or worry crossing a woman's brow
   like cloud shadow troubling a wheatfield,
as if she were remembering a stove
on at home, the child left
too long alone.

THE INVISIBLE STENOGRAPHER STROLLS
THROUGH THE PUBLIC GARDENS

past the war hero's bronze horse,
lush patina of tendon and flank stopped mid-stride
before anemone blossoms swaying on waist high stems,
small bowls in which drunken bees feed
on the last meal of the season.

Soon the golden, fan-shaped leaves
of the gingko will litter the ground, *living fossil*
cultivated by 8th century Chinese temple priests
while the wine loving poet Li-Po, *Exiled Immortal,*
wandered between princes and provinces.

Before too long she'll watch clouds of steam
unfurl from the horse's arched nostrils
as he stomps in the snow. She reassures him
he'll be among those who survive the winter
if history has anything to say.

THE INVISIBLE STENOGRAPHER LISTENS TO THE DEAD

Some nights they come to her, voices
calling from the edge of sleep, plaintive, distressed,
a faceless chorus discontent with how they fared
in the annals of history, the general protesting the victory
gone unnoticed, the diva insisting it was she
who sang like an angel, the mother still weeping
for losses too large to be held in the words she was allowed.

Where are the others, those contented
with how they are known now—the simple facts of a life,
the chain of memories, a few lines from a letter, a small invention perhaps;
and those for whom that was never important,
under whose care someone else flourished.

imagines walking in up to her neck,
white robe billowing about her, *Alleluia, Amen,*
though she's not fussy about theology, she'd welcome
a water spirit disguised as a fish caressing her thigh,
or the sight of Ho Po, god of the Yellow River,
sauntering along the shore, singing about a heron
watching a boat of fishermen go by.

So what if while underwater she excuses herself
from the annals of history? Wasn't it a school
of minnows that taught the philosopher
to re-arrange the world?

From the heron she'll observe
the necessity of death. Perhaps floating downstream
in an eddy of sticks she'll take time to rewrite
the history of nonbeing.

Isn't the scribbling of sunlight on water,
eloquent alarm startling the brown trout
back to the shadowed bank,
its own treatise on salvation?

THE INVISIBLE STENOGRAPHER IS TEMPTED

to change the record,
add a flourish of her own—

After the battle, the sky faded to a tourmaline wash—

for who'd know, she's mastered them all,
cuneiform, Sanskrit, calligraphy
in *Orchid Pavilion Style* . . .

Erase what must be mistakes.
The mother and father trading their children
for a sack of wheat. *We were hungry,* they said.

She hunches over her desk, humming
a snatch of Mahler, eyes glowing
above a fury of strokes.

THE INVISIBLE STENOGRAPHER DRIFTS BACK
TO THE LIBRARY AT ALEXANDRIA,

to its smoke and scattered ash, burnt papyrus scrolls
long ago become Namibian sand, soil of the Hebrides,
poppies, cotton gowns, a salamander's tail.

She imagines these particles reassembling
in a universe that remembers itself,
lost histories, theorems,
a poet's words.

Giddy at the thought of it, she closes her eyes:
head shaved, a shapeless tunic
falling from her shoulders, at first glance
she's another young scholar or scribe, a lovely boy
listening to the great ones.

She lifts her head toward the Nile.
Slender feluccas and barges of wheat
glide on water tinctured with pink and gold.
Soon the Lighthouse on Pharos will blaze seaward.
Citizens recline on the roofs of their city, wondering
when this age will be done, wine at their lips.

THE INVISIBLE STENOGRAPHER ON HER KNEES

I wanted to be a text of fire,
not what the data said, the figures and facts.
I pitied your human beings, saw how they fretted
over every petty detail when all they wanted
was to have loved more than they did.

Force field of compassion,
purveyor of cosmic dust, lift them up—
mist from the field's stubble.

ACKNOWLEDGMENTS

Beloit Poetry Journal: "Still Life: Nearly Reclining Woman, Settee and Leaning Axe"

The Christian Century: "After So Much Darkness" and "Sometimes I Wish the Rain"

The Georgia Review: "Father to Son" and "Morning Glories"

Image: "Consider," "Good Friday" (published in its original form as "In That Hour"), "The Man In the Next Pew," "To Begin With," "Once" and "When I Decide To Pray Again It Won't Be Words Strung in a Line"

The Journal: "Lines for My Father," "Fantazia *Upon One Note*," and "Fugue of the Long Trace"

The Midwest Quarterly: "Nights, Alone, in Her Chair" and "Why We Do Not Cut Down the Meadow"

Rattle: "The Invisible Stenographer Listens to the Dead," "The Invisible Stenographer Plays the Violin," "The Invisible Stenographer Rediscovers the Wheel," and "The Wind Refuses to Forget" (formerly titled "Relic")

River Styx: "Moss"

The Sewanee Review: "Letter From Mary to John" and "This Day"

Shenandoah: "To Clara, a Rehearsal"

The Southern Humanities Review: "Climbing Out of Eden" and "Imagine a Great Tenderness"

ABOUT THE AUTHOR

Kathleen A. Wakefield's book *Notations on the Visible World* (2000) won the 1999 Anhinga Prize for Poetry and was a recipient of the University of Rochester Lillian Fairchild Award. She has received grants from the New York State Foundation for the Arts, the Constance Saltonstall Foundation, and Mount Holyoke College. She taught creative writing at the Eastman School of Music and the University of Rochester and has worked as a poet-in-the-schools.